A Trapdoor, A Rupture, Something with Kinks

poems by

Laurie Rosenblatt

Finishing Line Press
Georgetown, Kentucky

A Trapdoor, A Rupture, Something with Kinks

For Mom

All things are engaged in writing their history...Not a foot steps into the snow, or along the ground, but prints in characters more or less lasting, a map of its march. The ground is all memoranda and signatures; and every object covered over with hints. In nature, this self-registration is incessant, and the narrative is the print of the seal.
Emerson 1850

Copyright © 2017 by Laurie Rosenblatt
ISBN 978-1-63534-098-3 First Edition
All rights reserved under International and Pan-American Copyright Conventions. No part of this book may be reproduced in any manner whatsoever without written permission from the publisher, except in the case of brief quotations embodied in critical articles and reviews.

ACKNOWLEDGMENTS

To the editors at *Third Space* and *Slush Pile*, thanks for publishing several of these poems.

Poems are such tenuous things. If not for the decades long friendship and mentorship of David Slavitt, these and my other work would never have existed. If not for the patience of an otherwise impatient man, my husband Leon Shapiro, my poetry would have wrecked on the rocks of my own doubt.

I owe Mary Ellen Geer, Jim Henle, Susan Jo Russell, and Oliver Payne for their support, fearless reading and insightful critique—credit them with what's good here (whatever remains is likely my pig-headedness).

Publisher: Leah Maines

Editor: Christen Kincaid

Cover Art: Laurie Rosenblatt

Author Photo: Laurie Rosenblatt

Cover Design: Elizabeth Maines

Printed in the USA on acid-free paper.
Order online: www.finishinglinepress.com
                also available on amazon.com

Author inquiries and mail orders:
Finishing Line Press
P. O. Box 1626
Georgetown, Kentucky 40324
U. S. A.

Table of Contents

A question, a moving target, a blind fold 1
Boston to Toledo; it starts with a trip home 2
Between take & take where is enough? 4
The date is easily misplaced 6
She is not delighted by unexpected visits 7
Discourse written by a cartoonist 10
I carry these birds in my mind 11
My mother tries out courage in the wreckage where now I
    rarely meet her 13
The landscape of future & meaning 14
A series of rooms all connected 15
Neither chicken nor blank 17
The gap can be measured in miles 18
Between far & I this holding on 20
The crooked bit is often a brink 21
Not the button looked for but the one at hand 23
I notice the weight of my wagging tail before tearing open
    her throat 25
She has forgotten today is the day of violent uprooting 26
Like someone else's life, something I'm being told 27
Carelessly turning over the restlessness of things 28
After red love, silence 29
Out-take 30
Ghosts of my mother 31

Introduction

My stomach dropped so fast it made my soles ache. Air expanded inside my skull until thoughts were tiny molecules separated by wide expanses of space. One word stood clear. Dementia.

Alzheimer's, Fronto-temporal, Lewy-body—it doesn't really matter which one. As it turns out, I've been losing my mother for years. She hid her confusion well. It must have been lonely. Now we travel treacherous ground, but at least we go together and so I dedicate this book to Mom.

I want to save her, to grab and clutch and hold on to who she was. So, these poems started with a diagnosis.

As I wrote about dementia's disrupted topology, I began to realize that the place we're born—with its history, geology, and indigenous diseases—insinuates itself into personal identity and the tenor of a family. My hometown, Toledo, Ohio sits on the edge of The Great Black Swamp—a trackless mire that spanned from Ohio to Michigan and Indiana. It was eventually drained in the late 19th century and is now farmland. For me, the swamp reflects the murky landscape in which my mother, brother, and I find ourselves.

With the help of Barbara Floyd at the Toledo University library, I found letters and diaries written by women living in Ohio during the 19th century. Facing death from cholera, malaria, autumnal fever, and childbirth, they write plainly about love, duty, grief and faith. Local physicians, some known as "swamp doctors" left books and diaries. Voices from these historical sources and other authors I've been reading began to talk to each other, an experience I imagine William Carlos Williams had while writing Paterson.

I wanted to include all these strands as a way of capturing the muddy domain that is dementia. With the help of my writing group, I found Haibun, a form practiced by Basho. His Haibun is a travel narrative interrupted by Haiku, it's a form that allows me to interleave historical and literary voices with my mother's story. I've varied the form, making a collage of voices. A few non-traditional syllabic and free-verse forms found their way in as well.

A question, a moving target, a blind fold

Between here & elsewhere, now & other-than I am pilgrim path, switchback, corpse road, drove road, blind alley, sarn, foil, & snicket: a track that runs back, both inside & out, a scat of history, birthplace, geology, & family. What happened breaks apart, shape-shifts, blends voices mixing mud with blood.

I went out to the fringes, picked a point and collected raw material. The making of a work of art really involves collecting. —Robert Smithson, 1969.

Here, is the story reformed. Its rough mosaic made from chipped & hammered bricks, blue-glazed, set in clay; my own talk juxtaposed with that of strangers. Not a real place, a nonsite, a transitioning space. The way through is uncertain.

A nonsite confronts the scale between indoors and outdoors, and how the two are impossible to bridge… —Robert Smithson, 1969.

We live it though. It's where the joyful meets the anguished O.

It's time to save it get it back get it right. It. The story. I write it to save my own damned life.

Boston to Toledo: it starts with a trip home

Toledo is in northwest Ohio, on the western end of Lake Erie, and borders the State of Michigan. The city was founded in 1833 on the west bank of the Maumee River, originally incorporated as part of Monroe County, Michigan Territory, then re-founded in 1837, after the conclusion of the Toledo War, when it was incorporated in Ohio.

Here on low land the family plot began braiding sickness, swamp, & skin.

The landing gear rattles & hums jarring me loose from thinking about Aunt Lenora, who, after missing two weeks at work, was found curled up under her Sheraton sideboard, starved, batty, smeared in her own shit. It's mom's turn now.

Related to intellectual madness is that disease of the mind, which has received from Mr. Pinel the name of "Demence". The subjects of it in Scotland are said to have "a bee in their bonnets." In the United States we say they are "flighty" or "hair-brained," and, sometimes, "a little cracked." —Dr. Benjamin Rush, 1812.

> Lost in her hive's honeyed cells,
> the queen bee wanders
> into a paper wasp's nest.

I squint out the plane's window trying to raise-up an old demon buried beneath the industrial farms. The Great Black Swamp refuses to rise.

The narrow peninsula between the Maumee estuary and the old bed of Swan Creek is the site of no less than three attempted towns—the first is Manhattan, the second, Toledo, and the third, Port Lawrence…From Drs. Smith and Perkins, of Toledo, I learned that from the commencement of settlement down to the time of my visit in 1842, the whole locality had been infested with fevers. —Dr. Daniel Drake, 1852.

> Numb, starved for a taste of awe, I cry "Swamp! Come!"
> Stupid wench. Would you call the wolf like a faithful dog,
> let it eat your grandchildren?

The wing dips. Interchanges shift into estuaries, corrugated steel barns blur into giant-oak ridges, light pummels windshields at the Jeep plant until fifteen hundred miles of moraine, dune, & glittering mire rises in unforgiving light. Like a judgment.

It echoes in the blood: oxen founder, horses sink in mud to the saddle skirts: slow oblivion drowns memory's terrain.

On Maumee, on Maumee, Tis ague in the fall;/ The fit will shake them so, It rocks the house and all./ There's a funeral every day, Without hearse or pall;/ They tuck them in the ground,/ With breeches, coat and all. —Anonymous, *Maumee City Express, 1837*

Between take & take where is enough?

1.
The months and days are wayfarers of a hundred generations, and the years that come and go are also travelers. —Basho

> Outside the window
> an aging woman pauses
> peers in on cookies
> studded with silver
> sugar spheres, buckshot of convex
> mirrors: her past.

2.
The solitary rhythm of childhood's Christmas Eve: awake late into the night, mom stuffs burlap stockings, fills them with carved pink soaps in the shapes of animals, with candy canes, nuts & wooden tops painted as lemons, pumpkins, blue squash. The live fir in the living room holds red-nosed reindeer & glass snowflakes out of reach. They dangle broad-minded & companionable with the skewed sequined angels my two younger brothers & I made at school. Wrapped around the tree's base, the hooked-rug it took mom three months to make—Santa, his sled overflowing with gifts.

She makes the daisy change; and everything runs like streaks of fire when she carves the beef. Virginia Woolf

Tom & Dan tile the roof of the gingerbread house with jellybeans. Taking out the scarred wooden rolling pin, I slip it into its cotton sock, grab a handful of flour, & run the barrel through my palm to dust it. The scalloped metal cookie cutters drop spruces, sleighs, five-pointed stars onto buttered baking sheets.

Where then is the break in this continuity? What the fissure through which one sees disaster? The circle is unbroken the harmony complete. Here is the central rhythm; here the common mainspring. I watch it expand, contract; and then expand again.—Virginia Woolf

In spite of all this & having just turned eight, I surreptitiously pocket pea-sized silver ornaments & plastic holly leaves with hollow red berries fallen from wreathes at K-mart.

It is beginning to feel a little like winter here these mornings...I should say Love in a cottage is all I ask for. Better so than in a marble palace for me. Perhaps this

is too sentimental for you. You must bear with it knowing that I don't often get sentimental. Roswell Chapin to Emma Turner Seville, OH 1873

3.
Thirty-two years on, the toy safe's bell hiccoughs in alarm. Inside are 3 painted wooden tops; a small soap carved into a bear (pale pink & rimed with its own dust); an ancient walnut whose nutmeat thuds against the shell (not the dry rattle I expect. It's baffling).

The things that I had hung over my shoulders tormented me first... —Basho

The date is easily misplaced

This Christmas Eve, my brother Tom is 7 years dead, dad has been gone 5, & the cookies are figments mom has convinced me to believe in. In the fridge, seventeen jars of olives crowd complementary bags containing make-up samples & bottles of salad dressing. "Twelve!" I shout maniacally waving the final vinaigrette trying to bully her back to herself.

...I feel disposed to look back for a few minutes, and contemplate, with painful and melancholy wonder, the immense changes in the human mind....How slender the tenure by which we hold our intellectual and moral existence! And how humiliating our situation from its loss! —Dr. Benjamin Rush 1812

> The short dry note in her voice, the cruel edge in mine,
> honeyed: conversation on a five-minute loop.

Nothing persists...I am afraid of the shock of sensation that leaps upon me, because I cannot deal with it as you do—I cannot make one moment merge into the next; to me they are all violent, all separate, and if I fall under the shock of the leap of the moment, you will be on me, tearing me to pieces. —Virginia Woolf

So, with my brother Dan's family due in an hour & the traditional rib roast on the lam, I call my husband to ask if year-old frozen brisket is safe to eat. Taking the first bite I discover two things: the meat is corned & salty rub therefore makes it inedible.

> The pizza arrives:
> a clumsy solution to
> a daughter's failure

Imagine our relief to find the white nylon-needled Christmas tree somehow standing in the corner. Beneath it more make-up bags & a four-foot carved Indonesian mask for my brother Dan. Christmas morning mom spots it leaning against the wall, "Your father bought that ugly thing. I've always hated it." Don't step on a crack.

> Tomorrow's Christmas angels turn to trash: berries
> shaken loose from false
> holly. How long can shoe-boxed relics hang onto
> childhood's magic?

She is not delighted by unexpected visits

1.
Facility tours. Doctors. Financial forms. Lawyers. A nine-month litany of minor events sets her up for the move from Toledo to Boston.

I get to Mom's before my brother Dan does. After a stiff hug at the door, she stalks back into the house her grimy heel flashing through the shockingly worn white sock. "*Tú no te callas, te tiras por las ventana!*" Since when does she speak Spanish? She's pulled it off, another false recovery.

> After flickering
> the incandescent bulb shines
> nothing but false hope.

From a part of the brain being preternaturally elevated, but not diseased, the mind sometimes discovers not only unusual strength and acuteness, but certain talents it never exhibited before. —Dr. Benjamin Rush 1812

She waits for me in the kitchen surrounded by cabinets covered with post-it notes: "Don't let them lock you up!" "I'm not leaving my home!" In front of the dishwasher she poses. Baby-doll blue eyes rolled up toward the ceiling, she whispers moving her lips, praying under her breath for my slow death. First you wish you weren't; then you're relieved you are. Adopted.

Display both casket and sword with paper carps. —Basho

Like singed hair, dendrites shrink back. Axons sputter like matches refusing fire. Line by line I struggle to recall that dementia drowns & defaces her.

> The Mystery Shack, The Biggest Ball of String; our
> childhood expeditions
> to local wonders die, fading into the eye's blue hole.

The Blue Hole is noted for its clarity, vibrant blue hue, and enigmatic "bottomless" appearance...Floods and droughts have no effect on temperature or water level....The water contains lime, soda, magnesia, and iron, and because the Blue Hole is anoxic, it cannot naturally sustain fish...it was known to Ottawa Indians, the first historical record is in 1761...Karl VerSteeg, George Yunk.

(Once my favorite tourist attraction it is now off limits to the public.)

2.
Toledo. Day two. Bird song before dawn. My bag holds no toothbrush, blush

mascara or eye-shadow.

> Bootless, I come to
> the realm of constant shifting
> where the stars release
> reason from its own
> weight, where thoughts lift away; drifts
> of fog in deaf winds—
> where is the meaning in this?
> Light footfalls did not wake me.

Naked hangers grin in a snaggle-toothed row. In my University of Toledo T-shirt I stand gazing at the sequential bare bottoms of dresser drawers then go downstairs to make coffee filling the mug stenciled with a unicorn surrounded by faded pink & purple balloons that I bought in college.

[A]nd there was some old rags of mine lying in the cupboard and Andrew asked me if they was mine, I said yes but I did not care anything about them. She said "take them along & wipe your old backsides with them." So you may know what a pleasant time I had of it, I am thankful it is all through with, she seemed to think the things were all hers. —Mrs. Mary E. Anderson, Toledo, Ohio, 1861

"Strange people keep coming in & leaving things around." Mom's eyelids flicker with brown eye shadow (hers is blue). She's got my sweater on, inside out. In view of her methods for cleaning toilets the possible fate of my toothbrush is something to think about.

> I pull out little drawers
> all of which are empty except for this
> desperate parody of me:
> a candle flutters in the mirror.

3.
Toledo, day three, I hear myself say, "What's this rolled up in a diaper?" This. A fork. Shelved right between Bleak House & Moby Dick. Alphabetically. She's clearly dropped a few marbles.

The first toy marbles (clay) made in the U.S. were made in Ohio by S. C. Dyke in the early 1890's....Some of the first U.S. mass-produced glass marbles were also made in Ohio, by James Harvey Leighton.

> Red opaque glass twists at the heart

> of this clear glass sphere: a coil
> of faces. One apes nursery rhymes,
> another bruises a knee,
> some old window cracked open admits
> the clang of bells, burnt oven mitts, night tears.

"Clean. Clean. Clean". She dubs three filthy towels. When I point out the make-up stains she says, "I do not know who you are." which I take to be spiteful. In this I am optimistic.

Gummed-thread & featherwork take our months & years. Even one day shakes the etch-a-sketch swiping a few scenes clean. And yet that evening watching Law & Order, á propos of nothing, she raises her voice drowning out the lead juror just as he reads the verdict, "How old are you Danny?"

She then muses en passant that her father died at just Dan's age. (Even when she invites him to visit it doesn't mean she doesn't wish to kill him).

> The heart, a dull blade,
> slides off the pear's smooth skin, turns
> on the grasping hand.

Holding the patent on a brand of layered quips she can still flay us though it's become hard to know when she means it.

> Every August that pain-in-the-ass
> raccoon raids my orchard, scarfs down
> the whole crop of Danson plums, pits & all.
>
> Gunned down, she drops from the branches, stunned
> but alive—her gutful of pits
> it seems is a really good flack-jacket.
>
> She and I understand the value
> in avid grievance collecting.

Her closing argument: "Life is a butcher shop. If I'm loony-tunes hang me by the feet from a doorframe." That's a good one. Comically picturesque. But then we do have a few slaughterhouses in the cow-full Midwest.

Discourse written by a cartoonist

In the dream mom works on an 8ft x 6ft canvas painting a diagram illustrating how to verify the quality of a match-strike in four instructional panels.

The first shows a wooden stick (red phosphorus head intact); in the next, a failed strike (grey smudge on one side); in the third frame, a burnt stub; the last a headless splinter.

I carry these birds in my mind

1.
As an olive has its pit, we should carry our dying inside us, a child's, small & straightforward, my mother's concerning itself with beauty in some aptly turbulent form. But she is less and less.

Familiarity with the disease allows observation of various terminal issues. These it seems reflect the illness rather than the character of those who suffer. —Dr. Daniel Drake, 1850.

Her dying like gravity should have presence but no particular characteristics assuming hers.

Shed not for her the bitter tear/ Nor give the heart to vain regret/Tis but the casket that lies here/ The gem that filled it sparkles yet. Tombstone, Ann Connolly, aged 22, d.1854, taken during the third great Toledo cholera epidemic.

> Her prior motivations guessed at by observing my
> defects; rippled forms caught in antique panes.

...distractions, inconsistencies, metamorphoses & distortions, these are indicative though not definitive, its onset may be insinuating or sudden. —Dr. Daniel Drake 1850

Jaunty whimsy & a laser temper no longer her possessions.

> Longing becomes a
> shaking fever of absence
> & faded presence

2.
Situated on a low-lying plain of the Maumee the town of Miltonville vanished completely...As did Providence...The only remaining trace is a roadside marker along present-day State Route 65, and a small hidden cemetery of mostly unreadable tombstones on a bluff across the road overlooking where the town was located. Medicine on the Maumee, 2013.

> Night confusions, doors kept carefully shut, my tarred
> window on the world. Though by comparison, this
> personal loss, feather-pale.

3.
Those who are sick have violated all the laws by which human beings exist... Ignorance, neglect of symptoms, intemperance, and filth, are the cause of nine-tenths of the disease."—The Toledo Blade, 1854.

> Dry-mouthed prairie dogs
> face the snake in their burrow:
> rage & excuses.

There was a little child taken ill in Perrysburg, and we are told that it was put in a bed in a room by itself, and all the family left the house, the parents looking in at the window now and then so see how it fared. As soon as it died they quitted the town, and the neighbors had to bury it: since which time they have all died.
—Mrs. Harriet Jukes Maumee Ohio, 1854.

(The past adopted, I fall prey to lost habits resumed, the voice & ways of my dead grow fainter, fainter—(never now to be fully understood.)

There is so much dread of the disease, that when a person is attacked few are found willing to nurse them, unless there are members of their family who can do it. Botanicals, blistering, bloodletting, mercury—(old crimes, blue silences, deep snow's pure breath drifting through a childhood room's secretly raised sash...strange blank-eyed malice-mother, it is me, it's only me).

My mother tries out courage in the wreckage where now I rarely meet her

"A woman with wickets in her head cannot be pharaoh of Toledo!" I tell myself she's simply misheard what I've just said.

There is an oblivion of names and vocables, and a substitution of a word no ways related to them. Thus I knew a gentleman, afflicted with this disease, who in calling for a knife asked for a bushel of wheat. —Dr. Benjamin Rush, 1812.

"A fit is falling apart on television," she says following me from the "kiteline" where coffee brews down the "ballgame" to the bathroom. I turn to look at her thinking "sun-swiped, windtackled" dear god, please make it mythic, this whisking away.

I am like the foam that races over the beach or the moonlight that falls arrowlike here on a tin can, here on a spike of the mailed sea holly, or a bone or a half-eaten boat. —Virginia Woolf

> I hold out stale cake
> in unexpectant fingers
> for grey-capped sparrows.

The body is so fallible. How can I expect it to house the soul if, when faced with the high-efficiency washer-dryer, her mouth opens as if on empty water into a silent O?

> We notice we are
> creatures when grief wets thyme left
> beneath the pillow.

I am whirled down caverns, and flap like paper against endless corridors, and must press my hand against the wall to draw myself back. —Virginia Woolf

The truth is sad & bloated. O for my dead father's hat, the old salt's oilskin he wears in the photograph, his face expectant, anticipates our laughter—I need it now to weather this shitsquall. But I am ungenerous, and so give nearly everything away.

Upon the lines of confusion/Upon the stones of emptiness/A great bitterness breaks open.

I meet as water with winter. I meet...

...the silence on the staircase, the silence in the next room, the silence high up under the ceiling...O Mother, oh you...You light a lamp, and that sound is already you...and you put it down slowly. —Rilke

The landscape of future & meaning

In a word, the mind in this disease may be considered as floating in a balloon and at the mercy of every object and thought that acts upon it. —Dr. Benjamin Rush, 1812

Animal cunning percolates up from her depths. Though the battlements & pasturelands of her character stand mired, she is still the unstable center I contend with. Ours is a sunken site unburdened by any focal point.

Persons who are afflicted are good-tempered and quarrelsome, malicious and kind, generous and miserly, all in the course of the same day. —Dr. Benjamin Rush, 1812

It seems she lifts a mask to reveal long-held hatreds. During a momentary truce I take out the photo albums. Turning the pages mom points to a picture of me taken when I graduated from med school. "That's my daughter."

Then who am I?

This belt, extending from the Huron River to the River Raisin abounds in green marshes, relieved by low sand dunes, which, at the present elevation of the lake may be regarded as irreclaimable. —Dr. Daniel Drake, 1852

> Fingering loose sheets,
> ink-sketches drawn years ago,
> she moves on, penning
> post-it notes—another fish-scale
> on the front door.

A child, I saw life flare in the black button eyes of a stuffed animal, willed the pupil to hold more than my reflected face, and yet.

…beyond the limits of the town, shows a wet or marshy surface, overshadowed with tall trees compactly arranged. This is the western edge of the notorious "Great Black Swamp," to be hereafter described —Dr. Daniel Drake, 1852

I need to redefine the limits of this, our disrupted landscape.

Without passing through, I entered it a short distance and am prepared to concur in all that has been said of its gloomy solitudes. —This description will do for the present.

A series of rooms all connected

The earth's surface and figments of the mind have a way of disintegrating into discrete regions...crystallizations break apart into deposits...crushing the landscape of logic...slumps, debris, slides all take place within the limits of the brain. —Robert Smithson, 1968

Stark stalks pricked-out. A wild field crisscrossed. At times, her thoughts are a lunatic's game of pick-up-sticks. Other times percolate between flat rocks. Like the ones he piled to lift the flowerbeds behind the house on Edgehill. There it is, the pepper scent of yellow tulip petals that brings back a husband, but leaves out his name. Night drizzles down on the man, his shirt incandescent against greying light. She hears from beyond his rolled sleeve's edge—rat-tat-tat-tat-tat—the nozzle sputtering in his hand.

> The maple seeds whirly-gig
> and fidget against
> the ribs of the shed's tin roof:
> noise like crumpled foil...

like the voice of that indifferent frost-grey sky the time palsied leaves skittered, spun, skated impossibly, miraculously on the creek. It visits her again, rapture. It makes no difference when she discovers the shore-bound ice, thin as wax paper, floating just beneath the surface. The leaves dance on water. She rushes into the hall, must tell someone, anyone. But it's gone.

> The key to the safe deposit box lost, the moth's rose-gold
> wings stay locked inside.

There are hours during which she suffers clarity. Her artist's eye measures the desolate expanse. In that hour the knock on the door that says time for lunch, or the aide's nightly visit no longer seem startling.

Then somehow having appeased the god of water & mud, she finds Frenchie, the short-order cook, a Pole who worked at her father's bar—Johnson's Aquarium Tap which was simply a board atop a large aquarium.

Up to Canada she rides with her brothers & sisters, their father singing "Susie, Susie sitt'n in a Chevrolet..." all the way to the lodge where he takes rich men big game hunting. (A taste for adventure stuck to mom's palate, so she married dad only later realizing that his exploits had a similar flair but lacked accuracy—an altogether different flavor of excitement.)

> In which blind did he leave the kids armed with their toy bows and target arrows? At dusk: the pines purple against white snow, then the doe.

Now she is six-years old jumping from the loft in her grandfather's barn. Hay fills her mouth and nose. She is drowning. Pain blasts her shoulders, iron bands crush her wrists when her older brother yanks her out. "Now *that* would have been the end of my stories," she tells the couch.

But, on a stoop in Chicago during a wartime blackout, she sits with her big brother watching the stars fall—one event still held tight in her fist.

> The last petals drift
> unnoticed from a stem left
> in the quiet house
> visited only
> by drafts: stories go unheard
> as she roves through her
> wild woods of elsewhere.

Neither chicken nor blank

"Look how green the trees are!" (This is her mother's relentless senile line). Roguishly mom delivers it with a comic's timing.

The gap can be measured in miles

However strange it may appear, it has been remarked, that there is sometimes an oblivion of the most recent, the most important, and the most interesting events. Of this I could mention several instances that have come within my own knowledge. —Benjamin Rush 1812

"It's like a gap" (her hand swings in an arc from left ear to right ear). "I know what I want to tell you, but can't get it out. It's very interesting really. I'm studying it."

My Dear Emma:
Sometimes the world becomes a desert and I am a doll stuffed with sawdust, where by I reach the conclusion that the earth isn't so bad after all since sawdust is the common stuffing of dolls, so I needn't feel bad about that in particular.
—Mary E. Anderson, Toledo, Ohio 1861.

> If one sentence could span mom's day, would it run shorter
> or longer than mine?
> Vinyl records, she and I play at different speeds.

On the whole, though, my minutes too lag outside telling. For instance, the way sunlight rushes toward the evening whiskey & escapist television, or a puff sends dust dancing off the books into the air (how many missing hours there?). Then I am sleepless, wheezing all night long.

> What was, what is, gone:
> pocket knife & snow day, years,
> a single sentence.
> The drafty baggage depot
> deaf to the storyteller.

Near the basket holding magazines I notice my boots point toward the window. Final item in the inventory of another day exhausted.

Days pass about the same. I have felt so weak today by spells…I have had a good deal of time to think of the closing year and the great shadow that has come to us as a family. —Laura Rhodes, Toledo, Ohio, 1889.

From St. Mary of the Assumption's steeple, a mockingbird belts out an intricate song, a pastiche of warblers, chickadees, robins, sparrows, jays, cardinals, & gulls. He wraps it up with a lawn mower's gnashing purr. A puzzling finish.

This day: a dancing
bird of paradise plying
bedraggled plumage.

Between far & I this holding on

Weighing methods for suicide my friend & I breaststroke from moored skiff to vacant mooring. Smells lift off the land—sunbaked seaweed, engine exhaust, marsh-reed, muck. Wind-stung grasses on the dune hum a monotonous tune.

Dime-size jellyfish fledge our legs but do not sting.

Although Alzheimer's runs in her bloodline, my friend delays, risks each year. I live blithely in my mind as if the brain is a thing apart. In this mom seems destined to prove me wrong.

        Siphon—this stark inlet stretching between land & island. Sun-rotten seaweed, truck exhaust, mud reek, rust:
the land calls out to us. We look for the seamark
for dying soon enough.

I miss mom's scrubbing, gut-plucking discontent. She consents like someone drowning.

Fiddler crabs mound earth at the burrow's lip,
sky blue & hyacinth
cloisonné shells duck in & out
now in sun, now shade.

Even if the moon keeps far away as possible, even so, water folds again & again on itself. This is the future of that hole, this tide creeping over her. Soon you will not find anyone there.

The crooked bit is often a brink

1.
I have put the quilt on the frame. I tied off a comfortable. The doctor was in and says it is a stage in the disease—a depression of the whole system—just take things easy. —Laura Rhodes Lamson Toledo Ohio 1892

When the rooms drift & shuffle or the keepsakes move furtive & quick inside her, or to meet the changeable weather when the oak & hornbeam having turned aside become alien for days; she layers Pashmina shawls over Irish-knit sweaters, eats the orchard's lumpy, worm-eaten fruit with undiminished appetite sealing herself to the sere land. She hopes to be wind-felled, struck down among apples, to be found crumpled on serrated leaves.

Each planet poised on her turning pole, with her ether of green and clouds of white and her waters that lie like fluid night...(end of entry) —Julia Gorham Commonplace Book, Seville Ohio 1830

I tell you this, about someone else's mother who had not wanted to end her days in an overheated room on bed-sheets soaked with urine—a question of integrity.

But her two daughters loved her.

Away! Away! This the wide, wide sky—the fears, the fields that before us lie. —Julia Gorham, Commonplace Book, Seville Ohio 1830, (The Song of the Stars)

2.
This morning drives the river to smash bottles against half-submerged stumps. Water & gust carry away clothes left on the bank by abandoned women.

> Deep river mud rarely sees the sky,
> so knows the empty fame of light.

...sin, suffering, and our sorrows!—and when have not these three words told the story of our life?—That spirit which looks into space with eyes of longing, which says to earth...(end of entry) —Julia Gorham, Commonplace Book, Seville Ohio 1830

Flecked by destruction the river glisters with good intentions.

3.
Pushing back the sleeves of mom's Irish-knit cardigan that I've slipped on

over my favorite wool sweater, I poke & startle mom's things with unfamiliar hands. My fingers pry, feeling for absent labels in braille that I should not need. I should know which are neutral & which cherished things. But don't.

> It occurs to the guest
> that within the sound of grey, a partial arc
> on the far left implies
> a clanging sea-swayed buoy:
> the smoke is shorthand for error.

A thought comes over us sometimes in the career of pleasure the troublous exultation of our ambitious pursuits:—a thought comes over us like a cloud, that around us and about us death—shame—crime—despair, are busy at their work. —Julia Gorham, Commonplace Book, Seville Ohio 1830 (Eugene Aram)

Because I have no daughter myself, I may still hope to drop unmolested among the apple trees. Until then I will keep turning week-old chicken into curried chicken salad.

Not the button looked for but the one at hand

1.
Toledo is a great glassmaking city. For half a century it has been what you might call the glassmaking capital of America. The town is full of glass companies. To a stranger they are a confusing hodge-podge. There are Owens-Illinois, and Libbey-Owens-Ford, and Libbey glass, and several more mixups of Libbeys and Owenses and what-nots—none of whom have anything to do with each other except that, in a round-about, left-handed way, they sometime do. See? —Ernie Pyle 1941

> I hold harsh words back
> wary of my capricious
> butterfly crafted
> from polychrome glass.
> Exquisite, fragile, her edge
> shines like steel filings.
> Cuts fine as those from paper.

Libby Glass does two things: It makes millions of drinking glasses…each one costs almost nothing; and it makes fantastically beautiful hand-worked glass… Some of the priceless pieces turned out in the last century leave you gasping, they are so outrageous. —Ernie Pyle 1941

Barrel-maker's widow + Irish ditch digger + French whore + Dutch drainage-pipe-layer + Algonquin slave + British soldier (& so many more)—a long chain of love's muck-ups start me out as a red-head mutt, in a year turn me blond. In the end, I'm dark-haired, thus, though no relation, looking more like dad. Although disappointed by these, ever darker, transformations, mom's smile in the pictures remains genuine.

Just think, if you yourself were to take a wheelbarrow load of sand, lime and ash—really nothing but a load of dirt, you see. Then you heat it to 2,600 degrees, and it gets fluid, about like molasses. And then, when you let it cool, instead of turning back to dirt again, as it should, it comes out clear and clean and brittle, like glass. My gosh, it IS glass! —Ernie Pyle 1941

When the Danish-modern shelves dad installed crashed down they formed a teepee under which I sat gripping my red Duncan yo-yo in a tiny fist & laughing. After all, I was prosaic & mass-produced.

> I would be firefly,
> hive beetle, grasshopper, moth
> made by hand from flame-
> worked glass: a coal-fired
> cullet, I have no

> sheath-wings to hide the glint of gilt.

Cures of patients, who suppose themselves to be glass, may easily be performed by pulling a chair upon which they are about to sit, from under them, and afterwards showing them a large collection of pieces of glass as the fragments of their bodies. —Benjamin Rush 1812

2.
So, my theory has sometimes been that it was to keep mom busy dad took us in. At other times I believe the picture book that told how it takes more effort to pick someone out than it does for a deceived secretary to conceive them. Especially if you & your brothers are accidents. And that we were.

> When water pours through the ceiling, it matters
> less that your buttons don't match

In the polaroid taken when I was ten-months old, I dance in a flounced dress, tipsy, & slightly off-balance, my expression tricksy & maniacal as if there's a joke only I suspect. I didn't speak soon enough to share that thought.

Of Joy. This emotion is attended sometimes with pain in the region of the heart, syncope, and death. —Benjamin Rush 1812

But then, one after another two boys who stay blond to look like mom came to stay. Dragged around by her yellow hair, my blue-eyed doll appears unloved. Still, if you get there first there is more to be had.

> We three, mismatched daisies
> that transposed the hour
> wanting to regret "from".

On Thursdays, I wait for my blanket to come out of the dryer. Have you noticed it takes a long time before a thing smells like yours?

> *The bin holding stuffed animals at Goodwill—*
> *all my friends in one place.*

Gyrating with Tom Jones while steam cleaning the rugs, she then cleans the bathroom swaying to the grind of the garbage disposal—I will do this same dance when cleaning my apartment fifteen years later. These similarities she chalks-up to "genes passed under the table".

It has been said, that people who live near the falls and rapids of our rivers are peculiarly liable to autumnal fever. —Dr. Daniel Drake 1850.

I notice the weight of my wagging tail before tearing open her throat

Frightened by the dream's vividness I expunge its bloody ending the next day the way most eight-year olds would by yapping, panting, lolling my tongue, chasing a ball with hysterical abandon.

    How words and dreams give breath to discord!

If our patient should imagine himself to be transformed into an animal of another species by transmigration, or any other way, ...our remedies should be accommodated to the grade of his madness, and the nature of the animal into which he supposes himself to be changed. Ridicule has sometimes been employed with success in such cases. A physician, formerly of this city, used to divert his friends by relating the history of a cure of a patient in this form of madness who believed himself to be a plant. —Dr. Benjamin Rush 1812

    A precarious
    equilibrium: the plum
    and its grafted twig.

Mom spent weeks soldering iron rods from papa's junkyard into a frame. On fishing line we strung brass hex nuts, bolts, steel set-screws, & gears painted in prismatic colors: either a gibbet or a hurly-burly galaxy of sorts. But is it love?

Lake Erie...is a long narrow body of water, an axis running nearly east northeast and west south-west. Its form is a compressed oval indented on the north side and elongated to a beak at its eastern extremity (Like an eccentric mirror) *—Dr. Daniel Drake, 1852*

    If you cannot look
    others will see it for you;
    the friction between
    a mirror dropped among gnarled
    roots and the reflected tree.

She is a landscape threaded through me, the place where scale is a question of interchangeable times and uncertain distances, a trapdoor, a rupture, something with kinks.

She has forgotten today is the day of violent uprooting

1.
In entering upon the subject of the following Inquiries and Observations, I feel as if I were about to tread upon consecrated ground…I thus humbly implore that BEING, whose government extends to the thoughts of all his creatures, so to direct mine, in this arduous undertaking, that nothing hurtful may fall from my pen. —Dr. Benjamin Rush, 1812

"You can't protect me from everything." mom says standing in her pink robe & silver slippers. She no longer walks on water or plays the female lead.

> Pennies, silver spoons
> hide in bathroom cabinets
> dazed in plastic trays.

By derangement in the understanding I mean every departure of the mind in its perceptions, judgments, and reasonings, from its natural and habitual order, accompanied with corresponding actions. —Dr. Benjamin Rush, 1812

Empty tape dispensers shuffle in the kitchen drawers. Inert in themselves they would have outlived her here. I stomp them. Squashing the tape under my shoe I roll the mess with my sole until tacky tangles barbed with plastic spines stick to the floor.

> This illness treated
> with blind tact leads to excess,
> to furtive jumbles
> in the irrational dark.

2.
Destined for my distant closet: the hummingbird pin, her mother's ring & two Japanese prints. Less has been signified by a return to my lists.

I am surrounded by a sense of language as matter…—Dr. Benjamin Rush, 1812

Into my carry-on bag slips the cigar box appliquéd in second grade that I covered with cut-outs from Life magazine of cells seen through an electron microscope. Luminous as fish scales they make a lacquered backdrop on which I glued photos of my grandparents, dad, mom, Tom, & Dan (complete with labels). The one of the dog lifts its edge. I try keys fitting no locks.

Like someone else's life, something I'm being told

1.
...as mountains collapse, rivers shift, and paths are renewed, stones are buried and hidden in the ground and trees age and are replaced by young ones, the passage of time and the changing world making me see, so far, only uncertain traces of them. —Basho

On shelves in the cedar closet: dad's microscope, his stethoscope & tuning fork, the Dictaphone that recorded his voice on blue plastic sleeves. He'd push the button on the microphone then tell tales about patients he'd seen that week. Outside the closed door I sat on the highest step listening to surgical sorceries, quests on which everything depends.

What will I offer to this day?

A woman reaching for the dishtowel after washing grapes in the stainless-steel sink, a woman thinking about her dad & how cold life went when he no longer paced-off the perimeter & her responsibilities loomed large?

A woman wondering what can be seen at an acute angle when time carries only the remains of leaves & cottonwood seeds, when yesterday reflects the child holding a dandelion under her chin wanting her brothers to see butter there, their second selves rippling over the brown creek, the water-spider poised, first resisting the current then yielding, the body a quick fulcrum shooting it forward.

The irrelevant detail—

an empty corn cob snapped in half stands-in for summer-sailing on Lake Erie; a boot blanched by salt-rind recalls tobogganing on Marshall's hill. I do not willingly part with the cracked rubber bucket,

or the metal bit lathered with the Arabian gelding's grass-spittle. Find me the denim jacket, the smell of saddle-soaped leather, dung, damp seed-spent hay.

Let me hear the ultra-fine etched lines play—hear dad talk to the Dictaphone. Breath on cold glass says I will give away

the microscope & stethoscope, the tuning fork & Grey's Anatomy; keep the palette knife & Parker pen, says that I will not hear his voice or recast his outline though I offer him this day.

Carelessly turning over the restless of things

1.
Mom says, "Get rid of it" pointing at dad's oil painting of a blood red rooster. "Get out of here," she commands the huge green monochrome acrylics he painted of Dan's kids. But, she won't give up the refrigerator-sized box of unmatched socks.

The longer this goes on, the hungrier I get.

The mind, in its distress from all the above causes...draws erroneous, or disproportionate conclusions from just causes. —Dr. Benjamin Rush 1812

2.
In circuits, mom searches, lost in the new apartment. Stripped from context she forgets. One rest stop along the highway of hollowing out is the limbo of assisted living, the memory unit another.

...the ice along the sea margin... a double perspective of past and future that follows a projection that vanishes into a non-existent present. —Robert Smithson 1966

Meanwhile, her empty bedroom is still saturated with her skin's emanations mixed with the sweet scent of her face cream. In the living room, bare hooks on bare walls, black scratches leave the marks of her resistance behind in these unquiet rooms where caring turned aggressive.

After red love, silence

Leaving me a latté & two orange scones, Dan starts the eight-hour drive home.

> A brother's departure seems violent and rushed even if
> you expect it.

My plane won't leave for hours. I wait through unfinished stories, slip around furniture that is no longer here.

> Hard dreaming inspires
> this wing-scrambled morning.

Wind moves through the hemlocks, a muffled roar like a river washing over boulders while below, beyond the low brick wall, is the shallow hole my father filled with poured cement intending to make a birdbath.

> A dark crater too heavy to move;
> let it be remaindered.

Robins scuff & ruffle drinking rain. The ruby-throated humming-bird hovers over the stain on the pool deck where the blue clay pot held a hibiscus for eighteen summers—he depends on it to survive the migration.

> There is nothing to eat in a sun-hunted house.

Pine boughs sift light through the sunroom's clerestory. Shade wavers across the white birch-wood floor that will not miss her footsteps. Among spangled needles regret wheels.

But the small cherry tree still clutches the iron ring from which the brass bell hangs.

2.
I return to the steel trussed camel-back bridge held together by bolts as big as my hands. Its flattened steel bands crisscrossed as tall x's between rail & arch. Below on the mud- bank, Tom & Dan fenced with sticks. Wet to the knees, I still see my brothers lunge & hit until dusk heads them home with intricate lies—a bully, the dog—held in their mouths, fragile as Easter's spun sugar eggs. That bridge is gone. Now low cement walls flank an asphalt slab. On the flood plain, the oaks & sycamores remain silent—as though I am already gone.

Out-take

"How are you, Mom?"
"I'm thinking of outhouses."
We laugh until we cry.

Ghosts of my Mother (generation loss)

The frame is empty now. But it once held a photograph that was larger than life as the hooks show.

*

Or was there never anything in the frame? It held the blank face of the wall—a Surrealist do-it-yourself work that presented a number of difficulties.

*

I recall a brightly colored picture. An exotic place. The most striking thing was the color. Periwinkle blue superimposed over blended rose and yellow, the mood hopeful, gentle.

*

No. It was a tiny black & white print of a woman standing on a boat in scuba gear. I think she wore a mask so I can't say who she was. That I am sure about.

*

I clearly recall red lips. I remember that. It must have been taken just before she goes over the side or her lipstick would have been washed off.

*

Selected from a lot of other possible images, it caught her by taking away & taking away until in that snap-shot she is a pillar of vertical black. Some touches of white. I remember white spread out above, perhaps clouds, and a white deck & cabin, the dark rectangular windows, everything black & white. Actually, I guess maybe a lot of white.

*

Rope. I see rope hanging over the side its frayed end flies in the wind. She is meant to get you to feel like that enraptured rope.

*

Wait. There was a white line cleated to the deck. Glossy, pulled taut. That's all I can think of. I don't know now.

*

Fins. She wears lime-green swim-fins. When you looked at the picture, those fins reassured you. I guess when I looked at it I thought it was taken before a drowning. I don't know why I worried about that.

*

I would say that the picture assumes a truth and a lie.

*

It's a color snap-shot in which she is happy & the man who took it is happy to show this joy. She is snapped in the moment when she is just exactly herself.

*

Those greys & browns. That's what struck me. Her blank eyes reminded me of ancient sculptures. Anything might be seen in them.

*

I remember two forms, the man blurred by motion. We can't see his face. We see his arms flung up against the sky. He must be tossing a net. That's what I think the picture is really about, the net.

*

I'm sure it was a salt print—sweat, sea-scurf and silver nitrate on paper pretending to be someone.

*

It was a cropped and framed photograve.